SANTA'S NEW CLOTHES

by Al and Eadie Felly

Copyright 2010

Limited First Edition

Published by
Kristin Mitchell Design, LLC

Produced by
Welsh House Productions, LLC

To order books: www.welshhouseproductions.com

Book design, development and layout: Kristin Mitchell Design, LLC
Illustrations: Tom Kelly

ISBN: 0-9828-0230-7

Printed and bound in the USA

In high school Al Felly enlisted in the Army Air Corps (1943). When the war ended, Al attended and graduated from the University of Wisconsin, class of 1949. After graduating, Al started in the flower business, creating Felly's Flowers. Eadie joined the company in 1965 and grew with the business. She held numerous posts including floor manager of the newly created 1-800-Flowers marketing division. During the 70s and 80s, Al and Eadie founded a high school in the new country of Belize, that still thrives today. Al continued as a florist until 1992. When he retired, Al started carving Santa Claus, they have become good friends.

Al and Eadie spend part of the year in charming Mineral Point, Wisconsin living in an old Welsh House Cottage on historic Shake Rag Street. They spend the other part of the year in Arizona. Al carves year 'round.

Tom Kelly is an artist with a devoted following. His artwork captures your attention, your imagination, your sense of humor, and then your heart.

Whether it's a painting, wood carving, or sculpture, Tom's art leaves an impression and makes your world a little brighter and a little happier. Tom also lives in Mineral Point where he has a studio. His work is available locally as well as in various other galleries.

DEDICATION

This book is dedicated to all children and to the freedom they enjoy, especially the grandchildren, Courtney, Taryn, Quinn, Jacob and Allie.

ACKNOWLEDGEMENTS

To Eadie for writing down my story as I came in from the shop with a new carving and new clothes — to Tom Kelly for his interpretation of the story in glorious color and to the talent and leadership of Kristin Mitchell, without whom this book would not be possible.

Al's carved wooden Santas, one for every month of the year and the inspiration for this book.

Meet Al, a woodcarver whose long days are spent
Carving all sorts of Santas to his kind heart's content.
Some Santas are smiling, some are big, others small.
But one thing's for sure, Al loves them all.

One day as Al whittled in his cozy woodshop
He spoke to the Santa taking form in his lap,
"Dear Santa, my friend, I wish you could speak,"
Al said, as he carved a plump, jolly cheek.
When suddenly, the figure sprang to life
Right out of the wood as Al put down his knife.

With utter surprise, Al asked Santa "Why?"
"You never asked me to speak, you silly guy!
All these years, dear Al, you've been so giving, so kind,
Spreading love through your Santas, leaving no one behind.
Now I'd like to return the favor to you
By sharing a wonderful story that's true."

Al settled in and Santa's eyes started to sparkle
As his story began of a beautiful couple.

Some time ago, in the early morning of Christmas Day,
Santa returned home from his deliveries in dismay.
With excitement, wife Emily swung open the door.
There stood Santa in soot from his head to the floor.
"Oh my poor Santa, you look so dirty and tired."
"Yes," he replied, "so much more travel's required!"

Santa was weary, that was quite true,
But his job's so important; what else could he do?
With many good children living in every direction
All minding their manners and learning their lessons!

With all the extra work and running around,
He looked different, he'd lost weight, he's now not so round.
He fits through the door; he can tighten his belt.
Santa couldn't believe how much better he felt.
"Emily, take a look, I can now touch my toes!
It won't be long — soon I'll need all new clothes."

Emily put her tired Santa to bed.
"Dear Santa, sleep well," sweet Emily said.
Then, she thought to herself, "Something must be done!"
Hmmm, as she sat down, an idea had begun.
Poor Santa's clothes don't fit anymore,
Looks like we'll be making a trip to the store.
But wait! I know, I'll make him something to wear
With grand fabrics and ribbons and all kinds of flair!

She crafted a suit made from velvet just right —
White and clean as fresh snow and berries so bright.
She wrapped it with love and tucked it away
For Santa to open that very next day.

Santa awoke in the morning from a long winter's night
Delighted with his new outfit; it fit him just right!
He raced out to thank Emily for her kindness and care.
He was so lucky to have her and the love that they shared.

January was here, wind so cold, stars so bright,

But Santa was warm in his soft suit of white.

The month went by and Santa busied himself.

He took care of the reindeer, he played with the elves.

Emily realized just one suit wouldn't do,
Santa needed a new one for February too!
She fashioned a warm, fluffy ivory suit
With red hearts for his love as a special tribute.

While Emily sewed, she started to scheme.
She would make many suits — what a wonderful dream!
The ideas kept coming, each new suit one by one.
She couldn't believe she was having such fun.

For March, shamrock green, with crisp little clovers for parades.
To celebrate the coming of spring as winter starts to fade.

April calls for light blue with pink and white flowers.
Just in time for drizzly, cool April showers!
The Easter Bunny welcomed Santa's presence,
To hide eggs and treats and to share his talents.

In May, Santa wore a soft Nile green suit
With bold black-eyed Susans and white daisies to boot.
Here come warm sunny breezes and brilliant blue skies
With white puffy clouds in every shape and every size.

June has arrived and that brought a new thought,
Pink is the color to remember those whom we've lost.
To represent hope and our wonderful lives,
Santa donned a handsome pink suit with ribbons and ties.

July, full of spirit, our flag we wave proudly.
Santa dresses in red, white and blue; firecrackers boom loudly.
With sparklers, sprinklers and picnics in the park
Night falls with magnificent, brilliant, bright sparks.

It was August and Santa was seen so much more,
His popularity grew and he was adored!
Santa's invitations to parties increased
To which he wore a tan linen suit with glitter and beads.

2

September came around with thoughts about school,
Girls and boys learning to read and follow the rules.
Santa wore a suit made just right for learning
Covered with numbers and letters... Emily's mind kept turning!

With Emily's talent for crafting bright costumes,
She made a Halloween outfit and left plenty of room,
For black cats and pumpkins and witches that twirled.
Santa looked amazing as he traveled the world.
He spent October teaching children to give
so that we all may enjoy the life that we live.

Then comes November and so do the leaves
Falling and spiraling right out of the trees.
Santa wore gleaming gold and fruits of the season.
We bow our heads in thanks for good reason.

December was upon us, the holiday season began.
Santa was in the spirit and started making plans.
He needed to be ready for his miraculous flight!
Lists were made, gifts were wrapped, hope the weather is alright.

The weather was so cold, colder than ever!
Would he keep warm or would he shiver?

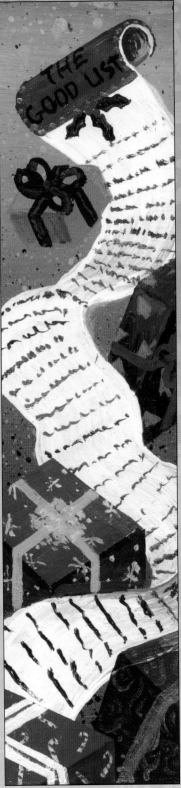

As Santa ran from workshop to workshop checking on gifts,
He realized as he hopped over huge snowdrifts;
A year had come and gone and he was still fit and slender.
How pleased he was with the year and his suits of such splendor.

One last suit to be made to finish out the year,
Not much of a challenge, for this one was clear.

Warm and cozy, red trimmed in white
To keep him warm throughout the night.
He gave Emily a kiss and bid her farewell.
"On Dasher, on Dancer," she heard Santa yell.

At the end of that long night, Emily tucked Santa in,
Wrapped him up in a quilt from his toes to his chin.
Good night. Sleep tight.

"So, my dear friend Al, that is my story to share
Of gifts given year 'round, good health, love and care."
Al looked down at Santa, a tear in his eye
So grateful to Santa as he said goodbye.

Santa started to fade back into the wood
And Al felt a feeling of peace, hope and good.
He slowly stood up to turn out the light
Locked the door to the woodshop and whispered "good night."

Good night.

You're not done yet,
There's more to do.
Go back and find a hidden picture or two.
Some are tricky.
Some are not.
Have some fun,
Have a lot!

'till we meet again...